My Cup Runs Over

Consecrated Unusual Prayer,
The Place Of Overflow

Prophetess Taketa Williams

My Cup Runs Over
Consecrated Unusual Prayer, The Place Of Overflow

ISBN 1-930276-09-5
Copyright © 2007 by Prophetess Taketa Williams
P.O. Box 7943
Columbus, Ohio 43207
Website: taketawilliamsministries.org

Unless otherwise indicated, all Scripture quotations are taken from the King James Version of the Bible.

Prayers and confessions are paraphrased from these versus unless otherwise stated.

Contents

INTRODUCTION

The Cup of the King

"And he went a little further, and fell on his face, and prayed, saying, O my Father, if it be possible, let this cup pass from me: nevertheless not as I will, but as thou wilt."
Matthew 26:39

Well over 2000 some years ago, Jesus' Kingship had to be confirmed and affirmed then validated in order to legally operate in His heavenly office down here on earth. He takes flight from His heavenly throne, steps down through forty and two generations, enters into the dressing room of a womb called Mary, wraps Himself up in flesh, passes through the portal of pain and finally is birthed out as our Majestic King.

Kings Must Be Confirmed

In order for one to be consecrated as a king generally another king had to confirm, affirm and later install them into their governmental position. In Matthew 2, we witness the confirmation of Christ by three wise men. These wise men were actually kings. Their divine assignment was to confirm Christ by establishing the truth regarding His Kingship. They followed the star that led them to the site of Jesus' birth. When the kings arrived to Bethlehem, they immediately authenticated and confirmed Jesus' kingship by bringing gifts before Him. They presented to King Jesus gold, frankincense and myrrh. Each gift's purpose was to bare witness to three different offices. The frankincense confirmed Jesus' office as a <u>Priest</u>. The myrrh confirmed His office as a <u>Prophet</u>. The gold confirmed His office as a <u>King</u>.

"And when they were come into the house, they saw the young child with Mary his mother, and fell down, and worshipped him: and when they had opened their treasures, they presented unto him gifts; gold, and frankincense, and myrrh."
Matthew 2:11

Kings Must Be Affirmed

Later, at the Garden of Gethsemane, Jesus is affirmed as a king. To provide affirmation is to state something solemnly before a court or magistrate. He is given a 'cup' by the Father and after the acceptance of His 'cup' He is affirmed by His friend Judas before the Sanhedrin Council, the officials and the magistrates. Judas solemnly confesses before the court of law that the one he kisses on the cheek is the King of the Jews. Had Jesus never embraced His 'cup', He would not have ever been able to be installed into office as an Earthly King. Letting the 'cup' pass Him by meant that His earthly destiny would have been forfeited and His kingship would have dissipated. The entire kingdom would have been handed over into the hands of the enemy had not Jesus laid hold of His cup. The power and privileges of the Kingdom lies in the power of the 'cup.'

Kings Must Be Installed

After Jesus' affirmation He is almost ready for installation. Prior to leaving Gethsemane there is another burst and wave of anointing that comes forth out of Him as He prepares to be seated upon His throne. Gethsemane was actually an Olive Press, therefore became the spot that the anointing was pressed and squeezed out of Jesus to equip Him for His next dimension in destiny. The press is so great that Jesus began to perspire and His sweat was like great drops of blood that fell to the ground. At that moment He received His release into His installation. He was violently escorted up Golgotha's Hill and brutally beaten at Calvary's Cross. What looked like a massive destruction was really a divine set up for a mighty demonstration. He is crucified with cruelty, wounded for our transgressions and bruised for all our iniquities. Though the pain is great and the agony is grievous at all cost He must endure. Through Christ's affliction, He is hung upon the throne and crowned with majesty. The cross became His throne and the thorns upon His head became His royal, kingly crown. The enemies of His life didn't know that they were installing Jesus into His office as King. Jesus asked the Father, "Forgive them for they know not what they do." While the crucifiers were mocking, a miracle was in the making and through their ignorance they helped it to come to pass.

"And when they had platted a crown of thorns,
they put it upon his head, and a reed in his right hand:
and they bowed the knee before him, and mocked

him, saying, Hail, King of the Jews!"
Mt 27:29

Every king had a cup and every king possessed a crown. The crown was the last thing Jesus needed to validate His position. It was on a rugged cross that our Saviour was officially and openly installed into His royal office as our Earthly King.

Five Meanings and Purposes of the Cup

-1-
The Cup Is the Place of Overflow

*Psalm 23:5 - Thou preparest a table before
me in the presence of mine enemies: thou anointest
my head with oil; my cup runneth over.*

Definition of Overflow...
To go beyond what one asked God to do

-2-
Inside the Cup Dwells the Will of God

*Matthew 26:39 - And he went a little further,
and fell on his face, and prayed, saying, O my Father, if
it be possible, let this cup pass from me: nevertheless
not as I will, but as thou wilt.*

Definition of Will...
Whatever God predetermined to be so;
the purposes and plan of God for your life

-3-

The Cup Is a Token of Favour

In Genesis 44, Joseph was bestowed a cup as a result of crazy favour being upon his life. He went from being a cupbearer to possessing his own cup. Rightfully Joseph wasn't supposed to have a cup because he wasn't a king - But Favour! Through this cup, he was able to partake of kingly blessings that he didn't even qualify for because he wasn't a king.

Definition of Favour...
An act of gracious kindness, to promote over
another, to bestow special privileges upon,
and to consider as the favorite

-4-

The Cup Is the Place of Activated Covenants

Luke 22:20 - Likewise also the cup after supper, saying, This cup is the new testament in my blood, which is shed for you.

This scripture says the cup "is" the New Testament (New Covenant) in my blood. Blood was an agent that activated and sealed (started and finished) covenants. In essence; the cup is activated covenants, released blessings, accomplished miracles, and completed promises.

Definition of Covenant...
The promises of God made to mankind relating to the
transfer of possessions and prosperity

-5-

The Cup Is the Cup of Blessing

*1 Corinthians 10:16 - The cup of blessing which we bless, is
it not the communion of the blood of Christ? The bread which
we break, is it not the communion of the body of Christ?*

The cup is filled with blessings. The Apostle Paul calls the
cup the "Cup of Blessing." The blessing mentioned in the
scripture that fills the cup is the Greek word Eulogia. The
Eulogia Blessing is actually a benediction on what was; an
invocation on what's to come; and an activation of what
already is (even as it is in heaven). When we drink from
the cup of blessing we bring closure on what's behind us
and walk into what's ahead of us. We also partake of the
heavenly promises that are above us.

Definition of Blessing...
A benediction on what was, an invocation on the benefits
to come and an activation of what has been promised

The Revelation of the Cup

One particular morning I went into prayer with such a strong desire and determination. I had purposed that I was not going to let go of the Lord's presence until He blessed me with a profound word that would change everything about my life and the lives of His people. I always make it a habit to stay connected with the very presence of God, but this particular day I was more driven than ever to reach heaven and to tap into His presence in a way that I had never before. Because of my endeavor and endurance in prayer, the Lord immediately began to speak to me. I could clearly hear him say, *"My people have been asking me for the blessing I gave to David in Psalm 23:5. I provided David with a cup that ran over. They want me to fill their cup to point of overflow and I desire to do it, but there's only one problem."* I said, *"What's the problem Lord."* He said, *"The problem is they have been asking me to fill something that they don't even have."*

At the very onset of my baffling, questionable thought, the Lord said to me, "That's right you have no cup for me to fill." I said, "Well Lord, if we don't have cups, then what is 'the cup' and how do we get one?" Instantly a Rhema word hit my spirit and the Lord gave me a revelation of 'the cup.' He said to me said, "The cup I'm looking to fill and cause to run over is the place of Consecrated Unusual Prayer." I began to go ballistic in the Holy Ghost because the Lord said that this very place would be our place of overflow. The revelation of the CUP (Consecrated Unusual Prayer) simply meant, No Cup – No Overflow!

If we don't experience the overflow of God in our lives, it is not because He doesn't want to bless us but because we don't pray Consecrated Unusual Prayers. God wants to bless us more than we want to be blessed. The word of the Lord says in Psalm 35:27 that the Lord takes pleasure in the prosperity of His servants. When this type of prayer is presented to God it welcomes the overflow of God to run continuously in our lives. When we get into this special place of prayer, God looks down into our cup of communion. His eyes penetrate deeply into our need as a sign that our problem and our lack has His full attention. He then pours out upon us not just what we ask Him for, but much more. Why? Because the cup instigates and provokes the overflow of God to be released in abundance in every part of our lives.

The presentation of our cup, tells the Lord that we are thirsty and ready for the overflow. When we go into a restaurant, the server's objective is to fill our hunger and our thirst. In fact, before they even address our hunger their goal is to quench our thirst. In order to accomplish this, they provide us with a cup. Without a cup, our thirst cannot be quenched. The server is not going to pour water in our hands, they won't dispense it in a bowl, and neither will they splatter it upon the table. What they will do is provide you with what you need to drink. So as it is with the Lord, He is not going to waste anything. Before He satisfies a need, we have to present something for Him to pour into. Our something that He's looking to fill is our CUP, an object of prayer.

Why does it seem like our prayer life is so hindered?

We often look at prayer as a task, an agenda item, or just one more thing to do. We must begin to look at prayer differently. Prayer primarily is not what we do, but it is where we go. Prayer is actually a place and must not be minimized to just a mere act. The word prayer in Greek is 'proseuche'. Proseuche was a place set apart specifically for the offering of prayer. It was a place in the open air where the Jews went to pray. This place was located outside the cities, and in places where they had no synagogue. These places were situated upon the bank of a stream or the shore of a sea where there was a supply of water for the purpose of washing the hands before prayer. This place of prayer was a familiar place to Daniel. The word of the Lord mentions in Daniel 10:4 that on the 24th day and the first month that Daniel was by the side of the great river called Hiddekel. What was he doing down by the riverside? Praying! This was his place of Consecrated Unusual Prayer. There were no synagogues for the Lord in Babylon therefore on the banks of this great Hiddekel River became the place. Prayer wasn't just what Daniel did, but actually where he went.

When Daniel went "there," God met him in an awesome way. At this place of prayer, when Daniel lifted up his eyes, His spiritual eyesight was "immediately" opened and he began to "instantly" see visions. Why was Daniel able to see so quickly and instantly? Daniels place of prayer was located at the great river called Hiddekel. This river was one of the four rivers that flowed out of the Garden of Eden and in the Hebrew this river's name means 'rapid.' Because of where he prayed, things had to happen rapidly and suddenly. A lot of times things don't happen as quickly as they should because we're not praying in the right place. See, we can pray the right prayers in the wrong place and end up with no results. People have said for so long that it doesn't matter where we prayer, as long as we pray. I beg to differ. Where we pray has everything to do with what God releases and how fast He responds. Sometimes quick car prayers won't do and rushed toilet prayers won't get you through. We have to set aside and mark the place that we plan to meet God. Divine visitations always happen at specific places. Abraham had a divine visitation from God when he went to sacrifice Isaac. The name of the place was called Jehovah Jireh because the Lord showed up in Abraham's situation and provided him a ram in a bush.

All throughout the scriptures we see specific prayer places mentioned. A place called the closet is mentioned in Matthew 6:6, *"But thou, when thou prayest, enter into thy closet, and when thou hast shut thy door, pray to thy Father which is in secret; and thy Father which seeth in secret shall reward thee openly."* The closet here is actually a secret place or inner chamber. This secret place of prayer provokes the "right now" hand of God. When we pray in the secret place, the word says that He will reward us openly. The manifestation of God's blessing in this verse is called the 'reward' and means to be given what belongs to the giver. Catch this – when being rewarded we are given gifts that belong to the Giver, who is a Gift Giving God, who loves to give gifts when we pray. When we get in the right place God will literally begin to share with us the very things that belong to Him. He will bestow upon us freely His divine riches in glory. Paul announces unto us a promise in Philippians 4:9, *"But my God shall supply all your need according to his riches in glory by Christ Jesus."* There is a key phrase in this scripture that must not be overlooked. The phrase that exudes from the word of God is **"according to his riches in glory by Christ Jesus."** This utterance helps us to understand where Christ retrieves our riches from before He releases them. It is clear here the measure in which God graces us and this measure is bestowed only according to His riches that are in glory. Anytime God begins to bless specifically out of His riches in glory, He blesses for the sole purpose of meeting our every need.

Power Point

We can pray the right prayers in the wrong place and end up with no results.

God's Riches In Glory

Riches of this world are obvious and we can clearly see the riches on earth, but imagine the riches that cannot be seen that are in glory which is Heaven. Glory is loaded with wealth and it is God's every intention to transfer these riches from Heaven to earth. In fact, the word 'Glory' in the Hebrew language is 'Kabod' which means wealth, riches, and abundance. Therefore, when God blesses according to His riches in glory, He retrieves it and releases it from His reservoir of abundance that saturates the atmosphere of Heaven.

Glory is the atmosphere of Heaven and according to Revelation 21:21, its' streets are made of gold and its' gates of pearl. Unusual abundance emanates from this glorious place. Revelation 22:1 says that pure water of life, clear as crystal, proceeds out of the very throne of God. The overflow that we desire originates and gushes forth directly from the throne of God. As we seek Him at the foot of His throne we receive a direct and immediate impartation of the overflow. The foundation of the glory is built upon fine gold and its atmosphere is saturated with pure abundance. The very thing we want released on earth is walked on by the inhabitants of Heaven. When we pray, we join in with the populace of this splendid community and begin to partake of the same prosperity and pleasures in glory. Heaven is loaded and enriched with immense wealth and enormous riches. Glory's glamour exemplifies our Glorious God. Through prayer we are rewarded with these same riches.

Solomon prayed a Consecrated Unusual Prayer. His prayer was so unusual in that he prayed different from every other king. Instead of asking God for wealth, he asked Him for wisdom. As a result, riches were bestowed upon him. *Riches are abnormal abundance and immeasurable increase of __external__ possessions released from the __eternal__.* How is what God has for us released from the eternal to the external? Hidden wealth from the heavenlies is released through consecrated unusual prayer and shows up when the weight of His glory comes upon us. When the glory of God shows up in our prayer life, at that very moment a divine transfer and transformation it takes place. What happens in the transfer? Earths' problems are being eradicated by Heaven's prosperity and before we know it a miracle will have happened.

When glory shows up, it's a sign that a portion of Heaven has come to earth. When glory appears, the reason why it is so weighty and heavy is because it arrives pregnant. It is loaded with the "More Than Enough" blessing of God. Remember, the 'Kabod' is wealth, riches and abundance. When we see the glory we must possess great expectation and expect our needs to be met beyond our expectations. The glory is the manifestation of the exceeding, abundantly above all we can ask or think. According to Numbers 14:21, there is coming a time where all the earth shall be filled with the glory of the Lord. When the glory of the Lord fills our earth, every crack, nook and cranny of our spiritual, mental, physical, financial and economical life shall be filled to the point of overflow. Then, we will begin to see the goodness of God flow in our lives like never before.

Chapter

The Secret Place

The secret place in prayer is a place where we empty out our secrets and receive an impartation of the secret mysteries of God. It is a place where we can be candid, free, and honest without embarrassment and fear of harassment. Jesus is our High Priest and it is in this place that we go to God in true confession admitting our faults, owning up to our mistakes, acknowledging our sins, pleading the blood, and ultimately receive forgiveness over our failures. It is through the power of our confession that we inherit divine possession. When we begin to confess to God areas in our life that don't line up with His word, He is provoked to release what His word says that we can possess.

> *Power Point*
> *It is through the power of our confession that we inherit divine possession.*

Confession always precedes possession. Romans 10:9 declares that if we confess with our mouth and believe in our heart that Jesus Christ is Lord and that God raised Jesus from the dead that we would saved – that is to possess salvation. What is it that we inherit through salvation? We possess eternal life, access into the heavens, a seat in heavenly places in Christ Jesus, victory over sin and death, and triumph over our enemies. In addition, we obtain the Sozo Blessing. Sozo is the Greek word for saved or salvation and it means to restore to health. We possess healing and restoration when we confess our pain and problems unto the Lord. The secret place actually provides us with an opportunity to empty out our pain and problems and receive the Lord's prophetic promises. Here the Master endows our emptiness, blesses our brokenness, washes our wounds and pours out on our pain. Here He heals us, thrills us, refills us and ultimately reveals us. The secret place is like a green room – a place of preparation that gets us completely ready to be revealed to the world.

Power Point

In the secret place, the Master endows our emptiness, blesses our brokenness, washes our wounds and pours out on our pain.

God wants to reveal His people in a major way. Romans 8:19 tells us why. The scripture says, *"For the earnest expectation of the creature waiteth for the manifestation of the sons of God."* This simply means that creation itself is assiduously and patiently waiting for the sons of God to be revealed on the earth. The earth is groaning to get back into the hands of its' rightful owners. The earth feels lost because it's not being possessed by its' proprietor. According Psalm 115:16 the earth belongs to us. The word says, *"The heaven, even the heavens, are the LORD'S: but the earth hath he given to the children of men."* God gave us the earth, but we have given the earth over to the devil and his demonic army. The earth is earnestly waiting for us to be revealed, rise up in power, and snatch it out of the hand of the enemy. When God reveals us, we gain power to walk as rulers in the earth. Whatever we speak to in the earth and on the earth has to obey our command. When we are truly made known, we can open our mouth in praise and the earth has to open up and bring forth our increase (Psalm 6:5-6).

The secret place sometimes seems like a darkroom. God gives us just enough light to see Him. We can't see anything else but Him here. We can't see our problems anymore. We can't see our perils and distresses anymore – all we can see is Jesus, who is the author and finisher of our faith. Distractions disappear and the noise fades away in the secret place. By the time we reach the secret place, what use to be an obstacle is now obsolete. We are not cognizant of what's beneath us or what's behind us, but rather our affections are now set only on those things that are above. What are the things that are above? James 1:17 describe these things as "every good gift and every perfect gift." The scripture says, *"Every good gift and every perfect gift is from above, and cometh down from the Father of lights, with whom is no variableness, neither shadow of turning."* Every gift that God intended for us to have is above. These gifts are good and they are perfect. They are set aside specifically for us and when our minds get in the right prayer position God allows these gifts to come to fruition in our lives.

Psalm 91 speaks of this consecrated place called the Secret Place. The word secret comes from the root Hebrew word which means to conceal or keep from being seen or found. It is a place of safety from life's hurricanes and a place of refugee from demonic tornados. The devil can't see us or find us in the Secret Place. God covers us with His presence and clothes us in His power. The shadow of His wings hides us. At the very touch of His wings instant healing begins to happen. Malachi 4:2 says that the Sun of Righteousness shall rise with healing in His wings. This type of healing refers to obtaining a cure for a problem and inheriting a sound mind. Secret place prayer provokes healing and seeking Him provides us with a sound mind. No type mental, physical or spiritual sicknesses, infirmities, or diseases can live in the secret place. The healing presence of God disallows them and causes them to be utterly dissipated.

The word secret in Psalm 91 is also used for the word convert. To convert is to transform or to change something into a different form for the purpose of modifying. When we don't seize our Secret Place our transformation process in God is halted and delayed. We become negated from being able to walk out the perfect will of God for our lives. When we are not transformed then we result to being conformed. We haphazardly conform to the things of this world and defy what God has predestined for us in the eternal world. Romans 12:2 declares, *"And be not conformed to this world: but be ye transformed by the renewing of your mind, that ye may prove what is that good, and acceptable, and perfect, will of God."* This scripture reveals that transformation and renewal of the mind allows us to "prove" or "clearly discern and recognize" the will of God for our lives. Without transformation, we gallivant through life unsystematically, unfulfilled, unfortunate and unaware of what our purpose is. Frustration and disappointment becomes our portion due to constantly falling short of personal goals because of lack of connectivity with our purpose and His personal promises. The personal promises of God can only be discovered when one identifies their purpose.

We must have a Psalm 91 experience daily. Notice the scripture says, "He that dwelleth in the secret place..." Dwelleth implies that this is a place where we must abide, remain or permanently stay. If we endeavor to live in this place, then we are destined to live in the overflow of God. The overflow causes our cups to run over. In the secret place, we are guaranteed to live in increase and the abundance of El Shaddai, who is God that is more than enough. Our cup presented unto the Lord in our Secret Place is our Consecrated Unusual Prayer. Prayer is the place that prosperity begins and promises of God are manifested.

Power Point

In the Secret Place, the type of transformation that happens is this – God causes our person to strategically line up with our purpose. *His glory supernaturally changes us, so that we can dynamically change the world.*

Chapter

3

The Power of the Cup

Throughout the scriptures, every time something monumental happened it was as a result of someone's prayer, a Consecrated Unusual Prayer. It was typically when a person got alone with God and began to cry out in desperation, that the Lord answered the supplication of His people. This particular type of prayer moves the heart of God. Why? Because this type of prayer, that I call "The CUP", provokes us to put everything else on hold and seek the Lord with all our might and with all that is within us. When God is made a priority, He will make us a priority and do things that we thought He was taking too long to get done.

Power Point
When God is made a priority, He will make us a priority and do things that we thought He was taking too long to get done.

A perfect example of the power that lies in "The Cup" is the prayer that Hezekiah prayed in 2 Kings 20.

The bible says that Isaiah had just prophesied a word to King Hezekiah. He told him to set his house in order because he was going to die and not live. The bible says in verse 2, "Then he turned his face to the wall and prayed unto the Lord." When Hezekiah turned his face to the wall his prayer became both consecrated and unusual. He consecrated himself by turning away from everything else and strictly concentrated on seeking the Lord. He prayed an unusual prayer because he turned his face to the wall which meant that his back was no longer against it. If you are ever going to pray effectively, you can't pray with your back against the wall. Turn around and face it. Don't run from it and don't attempt to escape - just pray.

Power Point

If you are ever going to pray effectively, you can't pray with your back against the wall. Turn around and face it. Don't run from it and don't attempt to escape - just pray.

A wall is symbolic of a barrier or opposition; therefore what was so unusual is that, unlike most people in trouble, Hezekiah turned and faced the force of adversity that seemed so great against him.

The scripture clearly said that the king "prayed." The word prayed in the text means to interpose or place a barrier or obstacle in the way. When Hezekiah turned to the wall, the wall now stood in the way of the spirit death and Hezekiah's life. There are some walls that we must thank God for. Every wall is not meant to come down because some are there to help protect us from what's coming after us. This wall in the text wasn't an ordinary wall. The word wall here in the scripture actually means chamber. So when Hezekiah turned and faced the wall he entered into a chamber and sought the face of God. In this chamber, the wall, Hezekiah found favour with the Lord. When Hezekiah turned his face to the wall and prayed, a miracle had to happen. The wall became his chamber and a chamber is the set place for miracles to take place. In 1 Kings 17:17-23, Elijah faces an emergency situation with the widow at Zarephath. She blesses the prophet as God commanded then she faces tragedy, her son dies. Elijah takes the dead baby and enters into the birthing ground for miracles. He takes the child into the chamber. It is in this high place that the baby is resurrected and comes back to life. Verse 23 says, *"And Elijah took the child, and brought him down out of the chamber into the house, and delivered him unto his mother: and Elijah said, See, thy son liveth."* The power of "The Cup" is that it provokes dead things to come back to life.

Prayer of Worship

Acknowledge Who I Am Before You Ask for What You Want

When Jesus taught the disciples to pray, He gave them instructions found in Matthew 6:9-11, *"After this manner therefore pray ye: Our Father which art in heaven, Hallowed be thy name. Thy kingdom come. Thy will be done in earth, as it is in heaven. Give us this day our daily bread."* The word teaches that the tributary stages of prayer should consist of worship. We must acknowledge who He is before we ask Him for what we want. It would be inappropriate for a child to grace a parent's presence only to get, without taking the time to give acknowledgement, show appreciation or even demonstrate reverence. The same goes with our heavenly Father. He finds it disrespectful for us to come before His presence void of the proper approach. All throughout the word of God, the Lord tells us how to draw nigh to His presence. A perfect example of one of the scripture's most suitable appeals is found in Psalm 100:2-4. The bible says, *"Serve the LORD with gladness: <u>come before his presence with singing</u>. Know ye that the LORD he is God:*

it is he that hath made us, and not we ourselves; we are his people, and the sheep of his pasture. Enter into his gates with thanksgiving, and into his courts with praise: be thankful unto him, and bless his name."

Power Point

As we proclaim who He is, we literally step inside of the same name we call Him.

Worship equips us to ask what we will and receive the desires of our heart. According to the scripture, worship is declaring who God is. In Matthew 6:9, He is hallowed which means holy and consecrated. When we endeavor to enter into our consecrated place we ultimately cross over into a special hallowed place. The scripture says, "Hallowed be thy name." According to the verse **this hallowed place is the name of the Lord, therefore when we pray we should run into the name of the Lord.** The name of the Lord is a strong tower and the righteous run into it and they are safe. As we proclaim who He is, we literally step inside of the same name we call Him. If we call Him Holy, we step into holiness. If we call Him Mighty, we step into might. If we call Him Great, we step into greatness. Every time we call on God's name we are elevated to another place in prayer.

Prayer of Worship

Our Father, which art in heaven, Holy is your name! You are El HaKadosh, the Holy God. You are holy in all your ways and I worship you in the beauty of your holiness. I exalt you LORD God, and worship at your holy hill; for the LORD our God is holy. You have given me a commandment in your word to rejoice in the LORD, ye righteous; and give thanks at the remembrance of your holiness. For it was by your holiness were you, Oh Lord, declared to be the Son of power. I proclaim that you are all powerful, you are Omnipotent. There is no greater power than the Power of the Highest. You are the Source of all powers that be. There is no power but of God and the powers that be are ordained of God. Your strength is surpassing and your might is magnificent. You are God who cannot be defeated and will not be overtaken. It is through the greatness of thy power do even our enemies submit themselves unto thee.

I invoke your presence at the very announcement of your name. Your name is Elohim, our Incredible Creator. In the beginning you created the heaven and the earth. The earth was void and without form and darkness crept upon the face of the deep and even in the midst of all the turmoil and catastrophe, your Spirit began to move on the face of the water. You then spoke into the darkness and demanded a manifestation of light and immediately there was light. What an awesome God we serve!

As I worship you, train my mouth speak like you. As I pray, give me the same creative power to speak things into existence. Through my prayer, anoint my words to call those things that be not as though they were. Give me legal authority both in heaven and in earth to decree a thing and watch it be established. As I worship you as the Miracle Worker, let miracles fill my mouth so that I may speak miracles into the earth. As I worship you as the Healer, let healing be released out of my mouth. As I worship you as the Prince of Peace, let the peace of God keep our hearts and minds in Christ Jesus.

Rhema Word – Worship

Hebrew Definition:
To bow down, to fall down,
to lay prostrate and to reverence

Greek Definition:
To kiss one's hand and lick
like a dog as a token of reverence

Scripture References:

1 Chronicles 16:29 - Give unto the LORD the glory due unto his name: bring an offering, and come before him: worship the LORD in the beauty of holiness.

Psalm 97:12 - Rejoice in the LORD, ye righteous; and give thanks at the remembrance of his holiness.

Romans 1:4 - And declared to be the Son of God with power, according to the spirit of holiness, by the resurrection from the dead:

Romans 13:1 - Let every soul be subject unto the higher powers. For there is no power but of God: the powers that be are ordained of God.

Psalm 66:3 - Say unto God, How terrible art thou in thy works! through the greatness of thy power shall thine enemies submit themselves unto thee.

John 4:23 - But the hour cometh, and now is, when the true worshippers shall worship the Father in spirit and in truth: for the Father seeketh such to worship him.

John 4:24 - God is a Spirit: and they that worship him must worship him in spirit and in truth.

Chapter

Prayer of Thanksgiving

Father, in the name of Jesus, I take this moment to give you thanks. I praise you because it is your will that I give you thanks in everything – both in good times and bad times. I rejoice in the fact that through the power of my praise that my bad times are shifted into great destiny moments!

You have given me a commandment according to 1 Chronicles 16:8 to give thanks unto the Lord, call upon your name and make known your deeds among the people. I thank you for all the wonderful things that you have done and for the amazing things that you're still going to do. I thank you for strength when I was weak and for food when I was hungry. I even bless you because you clothed me when I was naked and fixed me when I was broken. There is nothing too hard for you and you have proven yourself to be faithful to me. Great is thy faithfulness, morning by morning new mercies I see. All that you've done and all that you are to me I recall to my mind therefore I have hope. It is because of your mercy that I am not consumed for they are brand new every morning. Thank you for your mercy and your grace that has kept me when I couldn't keep myself.

Lord, I appreciate you for your faithfulness and commitment to fulfill your promises. Indeed you are a keeper of your word. You are not a man that you should lie, neither the son of man that you should repent. Have you not said and shall you not do it and have you not spoken it and shall you not make it good? Not a tittle of your word has ever fallen to the ground. Your word is sure and steadfast. It is proven, tested and tried. It has already ready been tried by fire seven times. Your word stands the test of time. Heaven and earth may pass away but your word will remain.

I thank you for the privilege to prophetically declare your word in prayer. When I pray, I praise you in advance because you will hasten your word to perform it. My heart is full of expectancy concerning the great things you are going to accomplish through the power of my prayer. I thank you because your word promises me that the effectual fervent prayers of the righteous avail much. I declare that I don't pray amiss, but I pray according to the will and the word of God. I thank you in advance for the manifestation of answered prayers as a result what I decree and declare in prayer. Your word says in Job 22:28 that if I decree a thing it would be established unto me and that your light (prosperity) would shine upon my ways. I decree that I break forth into divine illumination that enables me to supernaturally see my next blessing and my next miracle that's waiting to happen. Every time I praise you I usher in the manifestation of your grace and obtain a release of bountiful blessings. In Jesus' name I give you praise!

Rhema Word - Thanksgiving

Hebrew Definition:
Hebrew word is Yadah which is a form of praise and a spiritual weapon; means to cast down, to throw down, or to shoot forth arrows

Greek Definition:
Greek word is Charis which means favour, benefits, bountiful rewards, and the proof of grace

Scripture References:
1 Chronicles 16:8 - Give thanks unto the LORD, call upon his name, make known his deeds among the people.

Psalm 69:30 - I will praise the name of God with a song, and will magnify him with thanksgiving.

Psalm 100:4 - Enter into his gates with thanksgiving, and into his courts with praise: be thankful unto him, and bless his name.

Numbers 23:19 - God is not a man, that he should lie; neither the son of man, that he should repent: hath he said, and shall he not do it? or hath he spoken, and shall he not make it good?

Jeremiah 1:12 - Then said the LORD unto me, Thou hast well seen: for I will hasten my word to perform it.

1 Thessalonians 5:18 - In every thing give thanks: for this is the will of God in Christ Jesus concerning you.

James 5:16 - Confess your faults one to another, and pray one for another, that ye may be healed. The effectual fervent prayer of a righteous man availeth much.

Job 22:28 - Thou shalt also decree a thing, and it shall be established unto thee: and the light shall shine upon thy ways.

Prayer for Protection

Lord, I come to you as a child of the King. I bless you because you are my Father; you are Abba and you are Pater (my protector and my provider). You are my refuge and my fortress and your presence alone protects me from the hand of the enemy and keeps me safe from devastation and death. I am persuaded that in my times of trouble I can trust and depend on you to keep me safe and secure. Even when the storms rise and the winds blow your word says that you are a refuge from the storm and from the rain. Your word also says in Psalm 32:7 that you are my hiding place and you promised to protect me from trouble. *As you hide me in your Glory, cause my life to disappear from the very sight of the enemy so that he will not even be able to detect me. Cause my visible being to become invisible in the adversaries sight.*

As I boldly stand against adversity and difficulty, my prayer is that you would surround me with songs of victory. Sing over me songs of deliverance. Lord, open up your mouth and sing a melodious sound over me. Put a song in my heart and heaven's melody upon my mind to keep me during this challenging and rough time. Just as the psalmist proclaimed in Psalm 77:6, I also call to remembrance a song in the night. For even in the night shall your song be with me and in my darkest hour it shall keep me. Indeed you are a keeper and you are able to keep whatever I commend unto you.

Though the enemy has come against me, I completely trust in your everlasting arms to rescue me. I declare that you will thrust out every enemy from before me. No enemy or foe can stand before thee. You drive out both the chariots and the horsemen and they run in a ditch. Every enemy spirit is immobilized and inoperative in every single part of my life. I am free from the wiles of the devil for greater is He who stands within me than he who stands against me.

I decree the blood of Jesus over my family, my home, my career, my mind and my body. No weapon formed against me will be able to prosper. The blood of Jesus blocks adversity, sickness, poverty and disease. I proclaim that there is power in the Blood! The blood covers me from the crown of my head to the souls of my feet. Through the blood of Christ, the spirit of death has to pass me by. I apply the blood to the doorpost of my body, my soul and my spirit. Lord, release life over me and rebuke the spirit of death and discouragement away from me. You promised in your word that you would preserve me and keep me alive and cause me to be blessed upon the earth.

The hand of the Lord is strong upon me and your glorious presence overshadows me. Hide me in the secret place of your pavilion and let not anything come nigh to harm me. I decree your peace, your provision and your protection. In Jesus' Name - Amen.

Rhema Word - Refuge

Hebrew Definition:
A place of escape; from a root word
meaning to cause to disappear

Greek Definition:
A place to vanish safely out of danger;
to flee something abhorrent, especially from vices

Reference Scriptures:
Psalm 32:7 - Thou art my hiding place; thou shalt preserve me from trouble; thou shalt compass me about with songs of deliverance. Selah.

Psalm 59:16 - But I will sing of thy power; yea, I will sing aloud of thy mercy in the morning: for thou hast been my defence and refuge in the day of my trouble.

Isaiah 4:6 - And there shall be a tabernacle for a shadow in the daytime from the heat, and for a place of refuge, and for a covert from storm and from rain.

Isaiah 49:2 - And he hath made my mouth like a sharp sword; in the shadow of his hand hath he hid me, and made me a polished shaft; in his quiver hath he hid me;

Deuteronomy 33:27 - The eternal God is thy refuge, and underneath are the everlasting arms: and he shall thrust out the enemy from before thee; and shall say, Destroy them.

2 Samuel 22:3 - The God of my rock; in him will I trust: he is my shield, and the horn of my salvation, my high tower, and my refuge, my saviour; thou savest me from violence.

Psalm 91:2 - I will say of the LORD, He is my refuge and my fortress: my God; in him will I trust.

Psalm 142:5 - I cried unto thee, O LORD: I said, Thou art my refuge and my portion in the land of the living.

Psalm 41:2 - The LORD will preserve him, and keep him alive; and he shall be blessed upon the earth: and thou wilt not deliver him unto the will of his enemies.

Chapter

7

Prayer for Peace

Lord, I thank you that you are my peace. According to Isaiah 9:6, you are my Prince of Peace. Your name is Jehovah Shalom, the God of Peace. I decree your peace in my mind, in my heart, and in my home. I command the peace of God to be still in the midst of my storm. Every wind that is blowing in my life that has not been sent by you, I ask that you would release a calmness and stillness to the situation.

I confess that I am free from worry, distress and anxiety. I cast all my cares upon you because you care for me. I lay aside every weight that would cause me to be cumbersome and overwhelmed in my thoughts and in my mind. I ask that the peace of God settles my emotions and anchors my soul in your rest. Grant unto me an assurance that all is well and that you are in absolute control. With a meek and humble spirit, I submit to your Sovereignty. You promised me according to your word that the meek shall delight themselves in the abundance of peace. I glorify you that your peace flows in my life richly and abundantly and that it surpasses all understanding.

I bind the spirit of fear and nervousness and loose your power, love and a sound mind. I command fear to leave now and I decree that my faith in you is secure. Free me from any carnality of the mind because to be carnally minded is death but to be spiritually minded is life and peace. I confess that the strength of my faith defeats the spirit of fear and that I walk in triumphant power. My prayer is that you would transition me out of the shadows of darkness and death and into my next place of destiny. Cause the very thing that I am faced with to work together for my good. I declare that everything that the enemy meant for evil to destroy me and discourage me that you are turning it around and making it work in my favour. As the God of Peace, your word promises me in Romans 16:20 that you would bruise Satan under your feet. Lord, put your foot on the head of the enemy and crush his very thoughts and intents to plot against me and my family.

I declare that the peace of God infiltrates my relationships and friendships. I rebuke the spirit of confusion and ignorance and release the spirit of wisdom and knowledge. Lord, you are not the author of confusion, but of peace. I dismiss every argumentative spirit and the spirit of anger. Allow the fruit of your spirit to manifest in me and be revealed all around me. Help me to live peaceably amongst all men – even those who mistreat me and do me wrong. I declare your peace fills my home, my job, and my whole day. Your word promises me peace within my walls and prosperity within my palaces. I receive the promise of your peace. Because I have your peace, I also possess your prosperity. For wherever there's peace, there's prosperity. Today I prosper and move beyond my struggle and into my next place of success. In Jesus Name' Amen

Rhema Word – Peace

Hebrew Definition:
Wholeness, completeness, soundness, welfare, contentment, safety, health and prosperity

Greek Definition:
A state of tranquility, exemption from rage, harmony in friendships and relationships, the tranquil state of a soul assured of its salvation through Christ that causes one to fear nothing

Scripture References:
Isaiah 9:6 - For unto us a child is born, unto us a son is given: and the government shall be upon his shoulder: and his name shall be called Wonderful, Counsellor, The mighty God, The everlasting Father, The Prince of Peace.

Psalm 37:11 - But the meek shall inherit the earth; and shall delight themselves in the abundance of peace.

John 14:27 - Peace I leave with you, my peace I give unto you: not as the world giveth, give I unto you. Let not your heart be troubled, neither let it be afraid.

John 16:33 - These things I have spoken unto you, that

in me ye might have peace. In the world ye shall have tribulation: but be of good cheer; I have overcome the world.

Romans 8:6 - For to be carnally minded is death; but to be spiritually minded is life and peace.

Romans 14:17 - For the kingdom of God is not meat and drink; but righteousness, and peace, and joy in the Holy Ghost.

Romans 15:13 - Now the God of hope fill you with all joy and peace in believing, that ye may abound in hope, through the power of the Holy Ghost.

Romans 16:20 - And the God of peace shall bruise Satan under your feet shortly. The grace of our Lord Jesus Christ be with you. Amen.

1 Corinthians 14:33 - For God is not the author of confusion, but of peace, as in all churches of the saints.

Ephesians 2:14 - For he is our peace, who hath made both one, and hath broken down the middle wall of partition between us;

Philippians 4:7 - And the peace of God, which passeth all understanding, shall keep your hearts and minds through Christ Jesus.

Chapter

Prayer for Increase

Father, in the name of Jesus, I thank you for being such a gracious God. You are El Shaddai, the Almighty God, who is more than enough. You are indeed the God of increase who desires to give your people not just enough but more than enough. Lord, I ask that you would release yourself upon me right now. Pour out the essence of your presence upon me that I may receive a full impartation of who you are – for indeed you are More Than Enough! Inside of you is everything I need. My desire is strong toward you and my hunger is extremely great for you. You said in your word that if I hungered and thirsted after righteousness that I will be filled. I am asking that you fill me right now. Fill every empty place, every void place, every lacking place and every lonely place. It is not your will for me to lack. In fact you said in your word according to Psalm 35:27 that you take pleasure in the prosperity of your servants. Because I am a servant, I have legal right to confidently confess that you are my portion in the land of the living.

Lord, I position myself to receive the increase that you promised me therefore I decrease. I humble myself under your mighty hand and allow you to stand and rise in me. Rise in me with power, wisdom, and might. Add your strength to my weakness and apply your revelation to my ignorance. Grant unto me supernatural wisdom so that I might grow in wisdom and stature and ultimately obtain great favour both with God and man.

I pray that you would increase and enhance my footsteps to walk obediently in your word with ease. Today, I humbly observe to do all that you have written. What you have instructed is well with me and for this cause I shall increase mightily. I declare that you shall increase my greatness and comfort me on everyside. No longer will I feel minimized and less fortunate, but today I boldly announce that I am maximized and full of potential that will release my fortunes. I am maximized over low self esteem, I am aggrandized over inferiority, and my faith is magnified over fear. I am more than I give myself credit for. All the while I didn't have a clue who I really was. Today, I have a fresh revelation of who you are on the inside of me and I have a clear understanding of who I am in you. I have been fearfully and wonderfully made and marvelous are your works. I am your handiwork and a designer original.

From this day forward, I absolutely refuse to minimize my existence. I have been increased because of the increase of your presence that you have released in me. I am no longer the less than but the greater than. I am greater than where I came from and I am greater than what I came out of. My destiny is much larger than my history. Beyond all my failures and mistakes that had a way of making me feel minimized, I declare that I have been maximized. I have been increased and released to walk in the greatness of God. The Lord in me is Great and greatly to be praised. Father, I praise you and

Power Point
My destiny is much larger than my history.

lift you up. I exalt you above all the earth. With a voice of triumph I extol thee in praise. Finally, your word says in Psalm 67:6 that when the people began to praise you Oh Lord, the earth began to yield her increase. I thank you that through the power of my praise that my increase is rising up out of the earth and treasures are being released from dark places to flow richly in my life. In Jesus' Name I Pray! Amen

Rhema Word - Increase

Hebrew Definition:
Produce or fruit

Greek Definition:
To grow and to become greater

Reference Scriptures:
Psalm 35:27 - Let them shout for joy, and be glad, that favour my righteous cause: yea, let them say continually,

Let the LORD be magnified, which hath pleasure in the prosperity of his servant.

John 3:30 - He must increase, but I must decrease.

Deuteronomy 6:3 - Hear therefore, O Israel, and observe to do it; that it may be well with thee, and that ye may increase mightily, as the LORD God of thy fathers hath promised thee, in the land that floweth with milk and honey.

Psalm 142:5 - I cried unto thee, O LORD: I said, Thou art my refuge and my portion in the land of the living.

Job 8:7 - Though thy beginning was small, yet thy latter end should greatly increase.

Leviticus 26:4 - Then I will give you rain in due season, and the land shall yield her increase, and the trees of the field shall yield their fruit.

Psalm 67:6 - Then shall the earth yield her increase; and God, even our own God, shall bless us.

Psalm 71:21 - Thou shalt increase my greatness, and comfort me on every side.

Psalm 115:14 - The LORD shall increase you more and more, you and your children.

Chapter

Prayer for Healing

Father I come to you in the volume of the book. With a loud voice I cry out, *"Bless the LORD, O my soul: and all that is within me, bless his holy name. Bless the LORD, O my soul, and forget not all his benefits: Who forgiveth all thine iniquities; who healeth all thy diseases; Who redeemeth thy life from destruction; who crowneth thee with lovingkindness and tender mercies; Who satisfieth thy mouth with good things; so that thy youth is renewed like the eagle's." Psalm 10:1-5*

You are the Healing Balm of Gilead and I ask that fresh oil would saturate every place that I hurt. Let the anointing destroy every yoke of sickness, disease, and infirmity. Heal me Lord and I shall be healed. It is not your will that I am sick, but your purpose is that I prosper and be in good health even as my soul prospers. I command my body to come into divine alignment with God's will for my physical, mental, emotional and spiritual well-being. I ask that you bless the fruit of my body and restore me back to the original state in which you created man. Man was created in your very image and your likeness; therefore transform me back to the wholesome and complete form in which you created me.

Lord Jesus, you were wounded for my trangressions, bruised for my iniquities and the chastisement of my peace was upon you and by your stripes I am already healed. Today, I apply the power of the blood and the power of the cross to my body, my mind and my spirit. The blood of Jesus cleanses me and heals me from all sickness, disease, discomfort, hurt and pain. I ask that your healing power would begin to bring closure to every open wound and unresolved issued that has me bleeding. Instead, activate your blood to the place of my pain. Your blood is a sealing agent so seal me back up as a result of afflictions and attacks that have come against me. Fix me and deliver me from the spirit of brokenness. Put me back together again, repair what's been torn down, and restore what I have lost as a result.

I speak healing to my physical life.
I speak healing to my emotional life.
I speak healing to my spiritual life.
I speak healing to my financial life.
I speak healing to my interpersonal life.
I speak healing to my intrapersonal.
I speak healing to my mental life.
I speak healing to my economical life.
I speak healing over my biological life.
I speak healing to my social life.

I am whole internally and I am well externally. I am whole naturally because I believe and trust in you supernaturally. I confess that you have risen today with healing in your wings. I proclaim that the brush of your wings has healed me, freed me, and made me whole. Now I take flight upon your wings of healing and soar into a place of total restoration and renewal. I no longer lie on my bed of affliction and dwell feeble in my basement of despair for thy servant has been made whole.

Lord, I repent for any and all sins that I have committed that may have provoked this illness and injury. Cleanse my heart and all my wrong with the power of your blood. I close the door to past hurts, old wounds, previous rapes, and ancient afflictions. I will not rehearse my prior heartache and I will not replay in my mind former miseries, but I will practice thinking on whatsoever things are true, whatsoever things are honest, whatsoever things are just, whatsoever things are pure, whatsoever things are lovely, whatsoever things are of good report; if there be any virtue, and if there be any praise, think on these things. Lord, restore virtue to the complete essence of who I am and allow me to live in the power of your might. Your word says that you give power to the faint and strength to them that have no might. I ask that you strengthen me with might in the inner man. Go deep to the core of my life and disperse your anointing. Let it burst forth then bring forth a major internal healing that will enable me to walk in my physical prosperity. In Jesus' Name I have been made whole! Amen

Rhema Word - Healing

Hebrew Definition:
Hebrew word Rapha meaning to cure, to give back a sound mind, to free from distress, restore to good health, to restore a hurt nation back to favour, and to repair after being hurt

Greek Definition:
To free from errors and sins, to make whole

Reference Scriptures:
Malachi 4:2 - But unto you that fear my name shall the Sun of righteousness arise with healing in his wings; and ye shall go forth, and grow up as calves of the stall.

Deuteronomy 28:4 - Blessed shall be the fruit of thy body, and the fruit of thy ground, and the fruit of thy cattle, the increase of thy kine, and the flocks of thy sheep.

Psalm 107:20 - He sent his word, and healed them, and delivered them from their destructions.

Isaiah 53:5 - But he was wounded for our transgressions, he was bruised for our iniquities: the chastisement of our peace was upon him; and with his stripes we are healed.

Jeremiah 17:14 - Heal me, O LORD, and I shall be healed; save me, and I shall be saved: for thou art my praise.

Jeremiah 33:6 - Behold, I will bring it health and cure, and I will cure them, and will reveal unto them the abundance of peace and truth.

Luke 9:11 - And the people, when they knew it, followed him: and he received them, and spake unto them of the kingdom of God, and healed them that had need of healing.

Acts 10:38 - How God anointed Jesus of Nazareth with the Holy Ghost and with power: who went about doing good, and healing all that were oppressed of the devil; for God was with him.

James 5:16 - Confess your faults one to another, and pray one for another, that ye may be healed. The effectual fervent prayer of a righteous man availeth much.

3 John 1:2 - Beloved, I wish above all things that thou mayest prosper and be in health, even as thy soul prospereth.

Chapter

10

Fill My Cup
The Overflow Prayer

Lord, I come to you lifting this cup back to you that you gave to me. Anoint my head with oil and allow my cup to run over. Anoint my mind and destroy the perception and deception that prayer is some boring, ritualistic, burdensome task. I now realize that prayer is not just what we're to do, but it is a place that we must go. Thank you for dra\win me by your Spirit to the place of prayer. I renounce the sin of prayerlessness and the spirit of the antichrist that tries to lure me from the place of prayer. I announce that I do have a stedfast and willing spirit to seek you and embrace your presence through the power of prayer.

I ask that you allow your anointing to flow like a river upon my head. Release a fresh outpouring of your spirit upon me and let the power of prayer rest heavy upon me. You promised me in your word according to Psalm 23:5 that, *"Thou preparest a table before me in the presence of mine enemies: thou anointest my head with oil; my cup runneth over.*"

I declare a mighty release of your precious ointment right now upon both my conscious and subconscious mind, my thoughts, my intellect and my complete way of thinking. Cause my cup to run over immensely, abundantly, and profusely.

I decree and declare that the abundance of God saturates and permeates every single part of my life. Because I am now faithful in my prayer life, you promised me in your word that a faithful man shall abound with blessings. Lord, make your grace abound toward me abundantly. Grant unto me your grace without limitation, without constraint, and without measure. Send down the Former and the Latter rain, not moderately, but copiously. Open up the windows of heaven and pour me out a blessing that I won't have room enough to receive. Drench me in the rain until I am completely soaked in your abundant riches. You promised that you would give me richly all things to enjoy. I declare that my dry places disappear and that the overflow of God appears. I decree a supernatural manifestation of superabundance. Now unto Him who is able to do exceeding abundantly above all that I can ask or think according to the power that works in me.

I thank you for helping me to establish prayer as a priority in my life and placing a strong desire in my heart to pray. I declare that my mind is girded up for prayer and my heart pants after intimacy in prayer. Prayer is a kingdom principle and must be practiced on a regular basis in order to advance in the Kingdom. I ask that you, through my consistency in prayer, would give me something I've never had, do something you've never done, and take me somewhere I've never been. Amaze me and amuse me as I live in the place of overflow. I proclaim that from this day forward that there's no lack in my house and no slack in God's hand as I continue to embrace my place of Consecrated Unusual Prayer. As long as I have a CUP, then I will perpetually possess the overflow of God. In Jesus' Name – Amen!

Rhema Word - Overflow

Hebrew Definition:
To saturate, to cause one to be drunk,
to water abundantly, to drench

Greek Definition:
To exceed a need, to go over and above, to do more than
is necessary, to do more than ever before; to do
the superior, extraordinary, surpassing, uncommon

Reference Scriptures:
Psalm 23:5 - Thou preparest a table before me in the presence of mine enemies: thou anointest my head with oil; my cup runneth over.

Proverbs 28:20 - A faithful man shall abound with blessings: but he that maketh haste to be rich shall not be innocent.

Joel 2:23 - Be glad then, ye children of Zion, and rejoice in the LORD your God: for he hath given you the former rain moderately, and he will cause to come down for you the rain, the former rain, and the latter rain in the first month.

Joel 2:24 - And the floors shall be full of wheat, and the vats shall overflow with wine and oil.

2 Corinthians 9:8 - And God is able to make all grace abound toward you; that ye, always having all sufficiency in all things, may abound to every good work:

Ephesians 3:20 - Now unto him that is able to do exceeding abundantly above all that we ask or think, according to the power that worketh in

58370694R10037